**Please return or renew book
by last date shown above.**

Rothesay is a popular port of call for the present *Waverley*, seen here in Waverley Steam Navigation Co. Ltd colours in the 1975 or 1976.

STEAMERS OF THE CLYDE
NBR & LNER

ALISTAIR DEAYTON

TEMPUS

First published 2000
Copyright © Alistair Deayton, 2000

Tempus Publishing Limited
The Mill, Brimscombe Port,
Stroud, Gloucestershire, GL5 2QG

ISBN 0 7524 2107 7

Typesetting and origination by
Tempus Publishing Limited
Printed in Great Britain by
Midway Clark Printing, Wiltshire

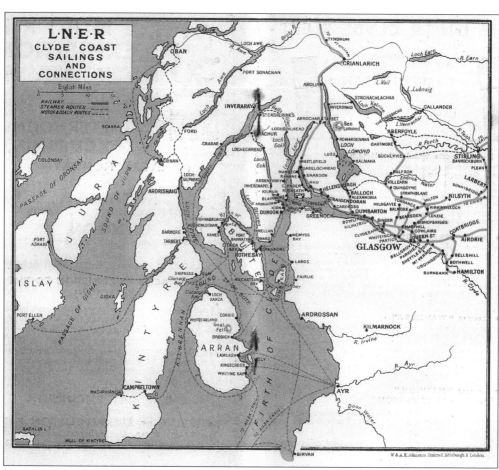

Map from the 1938 summer LNER timetable.

Contents

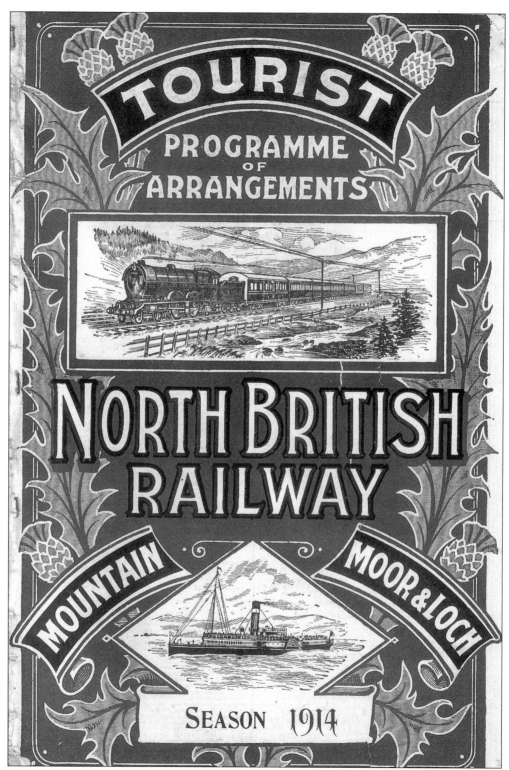

Cover of North British Railway *Tourist Programme of Arrangements for Season 1914.*

Introduction

In 1812, the *Comet*, on the first commercial steamship service in Europe, connected the town of Helensburgh with Glasgow. In 1858 the Glasgow, Dumbarton & Helensburgh Railway reached Helensburgh. This company was taken over by the Edinburgh & Glasgow Railway on 1 August 1862. On 31 July 1865 the Edinburgh & Glasgow Railway was itself taken over by the North British Railway, which two years earlier had formed a ship-owning subsidiary, the North British Steam Packet Company, to operate steamers from Silloth on the Solway.

In early 1866 the North British Steam Packet Company ordered two large, two-funnelled saloon paddle steamers from Messrs A. & J. Inglis. These were duly named *Meg Merrilies* and *Dandie Dinmont*, thus initiating a style of nomenclature after characters in Sir Walter Scott's novels, which was followed, with one exception, right up to 1947.

In summer 1866 these steamers were placed on a new route from Helensburgh to Ardrishaig, in competition with Hutcheson's established *Iona* service all the way from Glasgow. The NB Steam Packet service, along with a shorter one to Rothesay, lasted until 29 September of that year, after which the service was withdrawn. *Meg Merrilies* may have operated in 1867 on the Granton to Burntisland run in the Forth, and was later sold to Turkey.

The *Dandie Dinmont* was laid up for the 1867 and 1868 season but, according to some reports, ran on the Forth in the latter year. In 1869 Clyde services were re-commenced by the NB Steam Packet: to Dunoon and the Holy Loch with the *Dandie*, and to the Gareloch with *Carham*, a small steamer which had been built in 1864 for an NB Steam Packet feeder service on the Solway from Dumfries to Silloth. In 1871 she was sold to the Dingwall & Skye Railway Co. for service from Strome Ferry to Portree, being replaced in the NB Steam Packet Clyde fleet by the *Gareloch* in 1872.

In 1882 a new pier was opened at Craigendoran, about a mile east of Helensburgh. This was directly on the railway line, and became the base for the NB Steam Packet Clyde fleet, these 'Craigendoran Steamers' being distinguished by a gold-lined black hull and paddle boxes, and red funnel with white band and black top.

The Rothesay service was re-opened, and the *Sheila* purchased in 1882 from Gillies & Campbell's Wemyss Bay to Rothesay fleet. She had been built in 1877 and in 1883 was renamed *Guy Mannering*. A second *Meg Merrilies* appeared in 1883, but she was not a success, being returned to her builders, Barclay Curle & Co., after the summer season as she was too slow. She was altered, spent the next season on Belfast Lough, and eventually came under the ownership of the NB Steam Packet's arch-rivals, the Caledonian Steam Packet Co.

The builders produced a replacement for the 1884 season, the first *Jeanie Deans*, and she made up for the lack of speed of the *Meg* by being one of the fastest Clyde steamers of her era.

Diana Vernon was built for the Holy Loch run in 1885, and *Lucy Ashton* followed in 1888. This latter steamer was destined to be the longest-lived of the NB Steam Packet steamers, lasting right into British Railways ownership. Her original single-cylinder engine was replaced in 1902 by compound machinery.

Lady Clare and *Lady Rowena* came in 1891, both newly built for the Gareloch run and for a new Lochgoilhead and Arrochar service respectively.

Five more new steamers were built in the 1890s: *Redgauntlet* and *Dandie Dinmont* in 1895, *Talisman* in 1896, *Kenilworth* in 1898 and *Waverley*, the first member of the fleet to have compound machinery, in 1899. This latter steamer was used mainly on day excursions, for example around Bute or Arran.

On 1 October 1902, ownership of the steamers was transferred to the North British Railway Company (NBR), which had that year obtained powers to run steamers to most of the Clyde piers. 1906 saw the arrival of *Marmion*, the first member of the fleet to have her bridge forward of the funnel and to have a full-width fore saloon.

The NBR fleet did not follow the turbine steamer trend of the first decade of the century, remaining faithful to paddle steamers. Shallow water at Craigendoran at low tide would have meant that a turbine steamer would not have been able to berth.

A further steamer, *Fair Maid*, was built in 1915, but she was a war loss, and never saw service for the company.

During the First World War, a boom was erected from the Cloch lighthouse to Dunoon, and sailings were only operated inside this, to Dunoon, the Gareloch and the Holy Loch. *Dandie Dinmont* and *Lucy Ashton* maintained the services, the other members of the fleet having been requisitioned as minesweepers. When one or the other was off for maintenance, MacBrayne's *Fusilier* or *Mountaineer* or Buchanan's *Isle Of Cumbrae*, originally *Jeanie Deans*, was chartered.

When they returned from war duties, *Marmion* and *Waverley* had been decked forward to the bow and *Talisman* and *Kenilworth* had full-width fore saloons. That on *Marmion* was not successful and she was laid up in Bowling Harbour after the 1920 season, re-emerging in summer 1926 with the high bow removed and a fore saloon aft of the mast, shorter than that which she had originally been fitted with.

These six steamers passed to the London & North Eastern Railway on 1 January 1923, as part of the railway amalgamation, but there was little change to either the steamers or their services.

In 1931 the two-funnelled *Jeanie Deans* arrived in the fleet. She had been built by Fairfields at Govan, and was notable as the first Clyde Railway steamer to be fitted with triple-expansion machinery. She operated on the Arrochar run and on excursions.

Another important addition took place in 1935, with the introduction of the diesel/electric paddler *Talisman*. She was a unique vessel in UK paddler history, but her original engines were prone to failure in the pre-war years.

In 1936 the LNER paddlers sported a new look, with then fashionable grey hulls.

For the 1939 season, sailings were considerably contracted; only *Jeanie Deans*, *Marmion* and *Talisman* were in service, and *Lucy Ashton* and *Waverley* were laid up. However the *Lucy* was pressed into service on the Rothesay run when *Talisman* broke down. and *Waverley* was moved upriver in September to A. & J. Inglis' yard for conversion to a minesweeper.

From 1940 until 1945 the ageing *Lucy* held the fort on her own, while the other steamers were requisitioned for war service. *Waverley* was lost at Dunkirk in May 1940, and *Marmion* was not worth repairing after being sunk at Harwich during an air raid on the night of April 8 1941.

Talisman and *Jeanie Deans* rejoined *Lucy Ashton* in 1946, a year which saw a return to black hulls, lined in yellow instead of gold and with brown deck saloons. The following season brought a new *Waverley*, a two-funnelled paddle steamer from A. & J. Inglis.

Railway nationalization in 1948 saw the end of the red, white and black funnels, which were repainted in the British Railways colours of buff with a black top, and vessels began to call at Gourock on most sailings from Craigendoran to Dunoon and beyond.

Lucy Ashton was withdrawn in 1949, sold to the British Shipbuilding Research Association, and her hull fitted with jet engines for experimental work on underwater hull design.

One of the new motor vessels introduced into the Clyde fleet in 1953, *Maid of Ashton*, was based at Craigendoran and *Talisman* moved onto the Wemyss Bay to Millport run.

During the fifties and until 1964, *Jeanie Deans* was scheduled for a Monday to Friday afternoon cruise round Bute, while *Waverley* offered a variety of day excursions. From 1960 to 1964 the two paddle steamers swapped rosters on a weekly basis.

The north bank railway line to Helensburgh was electrified in November 1960, but the growth in private car ownership meant that the market for steamer cruises was already in decline. *Jeanie Deans* was withdrawn at the end of the 1964 season, and was sold to the Thames, where she sailed as *Queen Of The South* intermittently during the 1966 and 1967 seasons, before being sold for breaking up in Belgium. At the same time the Ayr excursions were discontinued and *Caledonia* moved to Craigendoran to replace her.

In 1965 all the Caledonain Steam Packet Co. steamers and motorships adopted a new livery, with a red lion on the funnels and 'monastral blue' hulls.

Talisman was withdrawn after the 1966 season and sold for scrapping.

In 1969 the Scottish Transport Group was founded, bringing the Clyde vessels of the Caledonian Steam Packet Co. and the West Highland vessels of David MacBrayne under single ownership. 1970 saw a reversion to black hulls, and 1973 the formation of Caledonian MacBrayne Ltd. *Waverley* adopted new funnel colours of red with a yellow disc surrounding the lions, and a black top.

Craigendoran pier was last used in September 1972.

1973 was *Waverley's* last season for the nationalized operator and the following year she was sold the Paddle Steamer Preservation Society (PSPS) for a nominal sum of £1. She re-entered service in May 1975, under the flag of the Waverley Steam Navigation Ltd, a company formed by the PSPS to own her, although sailings are operated by a company called Waverley Excursions Ltd. She was based at Glasgow from Friday to Sunday and at Ayr from Monday to Thursday. She regained the NB Steam Packet red-white-black funnel colours and gained a lot of popular support in the West of Scotland.

1977 saw her first foray outside the Firth of Clyde, with a few days operating out of Liverpool early in the season. On 15 July of that year she hit the headlines when she grounded on the Gantock rocks off Dunoon. She was pulled off and repaired, returning to service later that summer. The small motorship *Queen of Scots* was chartered for a few weeks to maintain a limited Clyde service. In spring 1981 *Waverley* was fitted with a new boiler.

The trips away from the Clyde eventually reached most coastal areas of the British mainland and Northern Ireland, and on three occasions she circumnavigated Great Britain, although sailings from the east coast, north of Ipswich, and from Northern Ireland, were maintained by the motorship *Balmoral* after she joined the fleet in 1986.

The motorship *Balmoral*, on arrival as a fleetmate in 1986, took some of the more unusual sailings, and the older *Waverley* got into her own routine: the Western Isles in early May, followed by a week or two each on the Solent and the Thames, a spell in June on the Bristol Channel, July and August on the Clyde, most of September on the Solent, late September and early October on the Thames, and a final weekend on the Bristol Channel in mid-October.

In 1999 she was awarded a £2.9 million National Lottery Grant for a major rebuild, and this was carried out at the yard of George Prior in Great Yarmouth from January to August 2000. *Waverley* returned to service on 18 August 2000.

Acknowledgements

The vast majority of these illustrations are from my own collection of Clyde steamer photographs and postcards, built up over the past forty years or so, since I was a child. Certain illustrations come from other sources as marked:

AB Alan Brown Collection

CRSCA Clyde River Steamer Club Archive collection of handbills, etc

DB Douglas Brown Collection

DD David Deayton photograph

GEL Graham E. Langmuir negative collection in the Mitchell Library, Glasgow

GUA The Andrew McQueen Collection in Glasgow University Archives

SC Rebuild photographs provided by Stuart Cameron, taken by Gordon Reid

SC2 Stuart Cameron

Sources/Bibliography:

Of the many books and booklets published over the years about Clyde Steamers, the following have been of use in the compilation of this volume.

Classic Scottish Paddle Steamers, A.J.S. Paterson, David & Charles, 1982

Clyde River & other Steamers, Duckworth & Langmuir, Brown Son & Ferguson, Fourth Edition 1990

Clyde Steamers (Clyde River Steamer Club annual magazine) various issues 1965 to date

Craigendoran Steamers, Alan Brown, Aggregate Publications, 1979

Craigendoran Story, The, George M. Stromier; Clyde River Steamer Club, 1983

Golden Years of the Clyde Steamers, The (1889-1914,) A.J.S. Paterson, David & Charles, 1969

HMS Aristocrat, A Paddler at war, Alan Brown and Richard Polglaze, Waverley Excursions Ltd, 1995

Merchant Fleets 26: Britain's Railway Steamers: Scottish & Irish Companies + Stena and MacBrayne, Duncan Haws, 1994

Talisman, The Solitary Crusader, Alan Brown, Aggregate Publications, 1980

Waverley; the Golden Jubilee, Waverley Excursions Ltd and Allan T. Condie Publications, 1997.

My thanks to Iain Quinn, *Waverley* enthusiast extraordinaire, for checking the manuscript for factual errors.

1926 handbill from Rothesay for what later became known as the Three Lochs tour to Arrochar, returning via Loch Lomond. *(CRSCA)*

One

Early NB Steamers

Meg Merrilies was the NB Steam Packet's first Clyde steamer. She only lasted for one season on the Clyde, as the ambitious service to Ardrishaig was withdrawn after the 1866 season. *Meg Merrilies* was laid up in Bowling Harbour, and may have seen a short spell of service on the Granton to Burntisland ferry service on the Forth. In 1868 she was sold to Turkish owners, for whom she sailed as a Bosphorus ferry until around 1915. This is a copy of a painting from a negative in Graham Langmuir's collection. *(GEL)*

NEW HELENSBURGH ROUTE
TO
AND FROM THE
WEST HIGHLANDS, OBAN,
Loch-Awe, Ardrishaig, Rothesay, Dunoon, &c.

☞ The most direct and convenient Route from Edinburgh, Glasgow, and the East Coast to the West Highlands. Passengers booked through to and from all Stations on the West Coast.

RETURN TICKETS ISSUED DAILY.

Excursionists to Ardrishaig are allowed two hours there before returning. The following is the Service now given to and from the West Coast, &c., by the North British Steam Packet Company's Saloon Paddle Steamers,

"MEG MIRRILIES" AND "DANDIE DINMONT,"

In connection with the North British Railway Company's Trains :—

TO THE WEST COAST AND WEST HIGHLANDS.						FROM THE WEST HIGHLANDS AND WEST COAST.				
Trains leave	A.M.	A.M.	A.M.	P.M		Coach leaves	A.M.	P.M.	A.M.	P.M.
Carlisle (via Waverley Route), at	..	..	8 15	..		Oban(fr Ardrishaig via Loch-Awe)	..	..	6 15	..
Hawick, ,,	..	..	10 23	..		Oban(fr Ardrishaig via Melfort),	..	..	7 45	..
Kelso, ,,	..	..	10 20	..					P.M.	
Melrose, ,,	..	..	11 4	..		Ardrishaig (via Loch-Awe, ..ar	..	..	1 45	..
Peebles, ,,	..	..	11 0	2 30		Do. (via Melfort) ar	..	..	1 45	..
Berwick, ,,	..	..	8 33	1 45		Steamers leave				
Edinburgh(Waverley Station), ..at	6 15	7 0	2 0	4 0		Ardrishaig, ...at	..	..	2 0	
Linlithgow, ,,	6 47	7 45	2 45	..		Rothesay, ...about	7 5	2 0	4 25	6 40
Polmont, ,,	6 58	7 55	2 55	4 40		Innellan, ,,	7 27	2 22	4 47	7 2
Falkirk, ,,	7 5	8 5	3 5	..		Dunoon, ,,	7 40	2 35	5 0	7 15
Glasgow(Queen-st)	7 30	9 20	4 0	5 15		Kirn, ,,	7 45	2 40	5 5	7 20
Cowlairs, ...at	7 33	9 28	4 8	5 23		Kilcreggan, ,,	8 0	2 55	5 20	7 35
Helensburgh, ..arr	8 20	10 35	4 55	6 13		Helensburgh, ..arr.	8 30	3 15	5 40	7 50
						Trains leave				
Steamers leave						Helensburgh, ...at	8 45	3 45	6 30	8 10
Helensburgh, ...at	8 30	10 45	5 5	6 5		Cowlairs, ...arr.	9 30	4 45	7 30	9 15
Kilcreggan, ar.abt	..	11 0	5 20	6 35		Glasgow(Queen-st)	9 45	4 55	7 30	9 25
Kirn, ,,	8 55	11 15	5 35	6 50		Falkirk, ...arr.	11 7	5 7	8 23	..
Dunoon, ,,	9 0	11 20	5 40	6 55		Polmont, ,,	11 15	5 37	8 22	..
Innellan, ,,	9 15	11 35	5 55	7 10		Linlithgow, ,,	11 25	..	8 33	..
Rothesay, ,,	9 37	12 0	6 25	7 40		Edinburgh(Waverley Station), arr.	12 0	6 20	9 30	..
Ardrishaig, ,,	12 5	..	..	..		Berwick, ,,	..	4 25	11 54	11 54
Coach leaves						Peebles, ,,	..	5 23	..	..
Ardrishaig(fr Oban via Loch-Awe)	12 30	..	..	..		Melrose, ,,	1 50p	8 12	..	..
Do. (for Oban via Melfort),	12 30	..	..	..		Kelso, ,,	2 43	9 9	..	..
Oban(via L Awe)ar	8 0	..	..	..		Hawick, ,,	2 41	9 8	..	..
Do. (via Melfort) ar	6 30	..	..	..		Carlisle (via Waverley Route) arr.	4 40	..	..	..

The Steamer calls at Colintraive, Tignabruaich, and Tarbert, both in going to and returning from Ardrishaig.

For full particulars of Cheap Tourist Ticket Arrangements to the West Highlands, see the North British Railway Company's Programme of Tours, which may be had at the Railway Stations, or from the General Superintendent's Office, North British Railway, Edinburgh or Glasgow.

Through Railway Carriages for the accommodation of Families, Pleasure Parties, &c.

Carriages to run through to and from Helensburgh, Carlisle, Newcastle, Melrose, Berwick, etc., can be obtained on application being made in writing to James M'Laren, General Superintendent, North British Railway, Edinburgh. **403**

A timetable for the first year of the NB Steam Packet's services on the Clyde, from Helensburgh to Ardrishaig in 1866, with train connections from Edinburgh and Carlisle (via the Waverley route) and onward horse-coach connections to Oban. (GEL

The *Dandie Dinmont*, seen here at Garelochhead, was a sister of the *Meg Merrilies*, also coming from A. & J. Inglis. Likewise she was laid up after the 1866 season, but reappeared on the Clyde in 1869, sailing from Helensburgh to Dunoon and the Holy Loch, and from 1882 from Craigendoran, until she was replaced in 1885 by *Diana Vernon*. In August 1887 she was sold to the Southsea, Ventnor, Sandown and Shanklin Steamboat Company, sailing between these piers until 1900. She was then laid up at Bembridge until December 1902 when she was towed to Holland for scrapping. *(DB)*

Few photographs of *Carham* survive, and none worthy of reproduction from her NB career. She is seen here at Strome Ferry while under the ownership of the Highland Railway Company. *Carham* was built by A. & J. Inglis in 1864 for services on the Solway Firth. In 1867 she was transferred to the Clyde to run a more modest service than that of 1866, and in 1871 was sold to the Dingwall and Skye Railway to run from Strome Ferry to Portree. In 1877 she was sold to Bournemouth owners, and in 1882 to Ramsgate owners, for whom she was renamed *Queen of Thanet*. In 1887 she was purchased by Liverpool owners and was scrapped the following year.

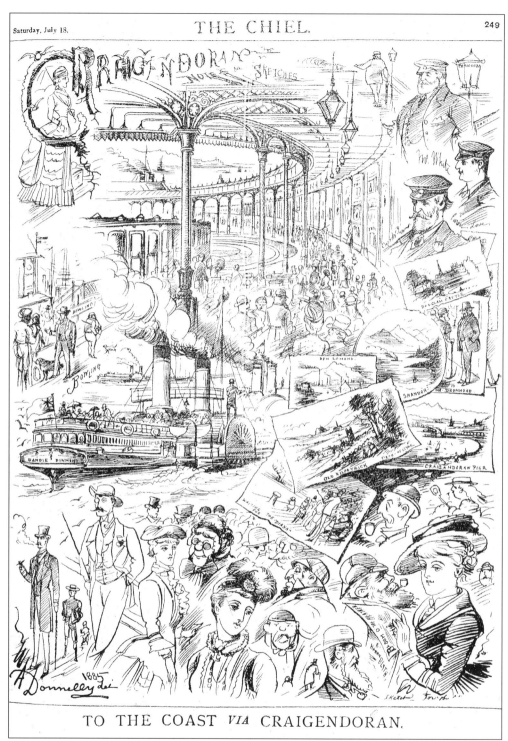

TO THE COAST VIA CRAIGENDORAN.

A composite sketch from a contemporary magazine named *The Chiel*, entitled 'To the Coast via Craigendoran', showing *Dandie Dinmont*, the curved bay terminal platform at Craigendoran pier used by steamer connecting trains, and some drawings of the passengers and crew. *(GEL)*

Gareloch was a raised quarter deck type steamer, built in 1872 by H. Murray & Co. of Port Glasgow, with 2-cylinder oscillating machinery from David Rowan of Glasgow, for the North British Steam Packet Co. service from Helensburgh to the Gareloch. This photograph of her approaching Shandon on the Gareloch dates from after 1883 when the NB Steam Packet adopted the familiar livery of a white band separating the red funnel from the black top.

In 1891 *Gareloch* was transferred to the Forth fleet of the Galloway Saloon Steam Packet Co., majority owned by the NBR, where, renamed *Wemyss Castle*, she served until sold for breaking up in 1906. In this illustration she is seen at Elie, probably in 1891 as regular calls there ceased after that season.

Sheila had been built in 1877 by Caird's of Greenock for Gillies and Campbell. She was the fastest steamer on the firth when built, was purchased by the NB Steam Packet in 1882 for the Craigendoran to Rothesay service, and was renamed *Guy Mannering* in 1883. She is seen here at Kilcreggan Pier in its original form, before she was rebuilt in 1891.

In 1892 *Guy Mannering* was fitted with an aft deck saloon and a small fore saloon, as seen in this picture. *(DB)*

In 1894 *Guy Mannering* was sold to Captain William Buchanan and renamed *Isle of Bute*. This illustration shows her in the river at Glasgow. In 1912 she was sold to owners at Morecambe and scrapped the following year after a collision with Morecambe Pier.

The second *Meg Merrilies* was built in 1883 by Barclay Curle for the NB Steam Packet's Craigendoran to Rothesay service, but was unable to make the speed of the *Guy Mannering*, and was returned to her builders as unsatisfactory after her first season. She is seen here in Rothesay Bay with MacBrayne's *Columba*, during the short period when she carried NB colours. *(GUA)*

After being returned to her builders after the 1883 season, *Meg Merrilies* spent a season on charter in Belfast Lough. She was then sold in 1885 to Captain Robert Campbell of Kilmun and ran from the Broomielaw to the Holy Loch. She is seen here in Campbell colours at Kilcreggan Pier.

In 1888 *Meg Merrilies* was re-boilered and emerged with a single funnel, before being sold in 1889 to the Caledonian Steam Packet Co., in whose colours she is seen here. In 1902 she was sold to the Leopoldina Railway in Brazil, operating local ferry services at Rio as *Maua*, until scrapped in 1922.

Two
Jeanie & Diana

In 1884, Barclay Curle produced a replacement for *Meg Merrilies* in the form of *Jeanie Deans*. The mistakes in the previous design had been corrected and the *Jeanie* was a noted flyer, reaching 17.5 knots on trials. She is seen here in her original condition without deck saloons, which were added in 1894.

A stern view of *Jeanie Deans* in similar condition.

Diana Vernon, also built by Barclay Curle, followed *Jeanie Deans* (left) in 1885. The two are seen here at Craigendoran pier.

Sold in 1896 for use on Lough Foyle by the Derry and Moville Steam Packet Co., *Jeanie Deans* came back to the Clyde in 1899 for Dawson Reid's Glasgow Steamers Ltd as the *Duchess of York*, offering cruises from Glasgow including Sunday-breaking services (GUA)

Jeanie Deans in 1894-1895, after her deck saloons had been added.

In 1904 *Jeanie Deans* was acquired by Captain Buchanan, who renamed her *Isle of Cumbrae*. In 1916 she was chartered to the Glasgow & South Western Railway fleet, and painted in their colours, as seen here.

During the First World War she was also chartered to David MacBrayne Ltd. She is seen here with a MacBrayne funnel. She was scrapped in 1919.

A side-on view of *Diana Vernon* off Kilcreggan, showing the deck saloons. This picture shows clearly the bridge across the paddle-boxes, which gave its name to the modern ship's bridge, with the helmsman standing on it.

Diana Vernon (left) passing *Shandon*, originally *Chancellor* of 1864, in Rothesay Bay.

31 BRIGHTON. — " *Worthing Belle* " *and Bathers* — LL

In 1901 *Diana Vernon* was sold to Brighton owners who named her *Worthing Belle*, running to Eastbourne and Worthing. This postcard view shows her leaving Brighton.

Worthing Belle ran on the South Coast until 1913, and was sold to Turkish owners the following year. She operated at Constantinople as *Touzla*, and was sunk by a mine in the Dardanelles on 30 August 1915. *Worthing Belle* is seen here departing Newhaven.

Three
Lucy

An early view of the *Lucy Ashton*, built by Seath of Rutherglen in 1888, with machinery by Hutson & Corbett. She was destined to be the longest-lived NB Steam Packet steamer.

Lucy Ashton trailing a large plume of black coal smoke with *Dandie Dinmont (II)* in the background.

Lucy Ashton flying the LNER houseflag.

In 1903 *Lucy's* deck saloons were enlarged and the sponsons rebuilt with windows rather than portholes. In 1908 a companionway shelter was fitted above the stairs from the fore saloon. Both these alterations can be seen in this shot off Dunoon.

In 1901 *Lucy Ashton's* original single-cylinder diagonal engine was replaced by a new two-cylinder compound engine from A. & J. Inglis. She is seen here in a postcard view leaving Helensburgh Pier. By this time, *Lucy Ashton* was being used on the Greenock-Craigendoran-Gareloch route, which she made hers for the remainder of her career.

Spring and Victoria Day Holidays at Greenock

Augmented Service between

GREENOCK and HELENSBURGH and GARELOCH PIERS

WILL BE GIVEN ON

Monday, 11th April and Wednesday, 25th May 1932

AS FOLLOWS :—

			a.m.	a.m.	p.m.	p.m.	p.m.
Garelochhead	...	leave	7 20	...	12 20	2 55	6 0
Mambeg ...	...	,,	7 25	...	12*15	...	5*25
Rahane Ferry	...	,,	7 30	...	12*10	...	5*20
Clynder ...	...	,,	7 40	9 30	12 35	3 10	6 15
Rosneath ...	...	,,	7 50	9*18	12 45	3 20	6 24
Helensburgh	...	,,	8 3	...	12 58	3 33	6 37
Craigendoran	...	arrive	8 10	9 50	1 5	3 40	6 45
Do.	...	leave	8 20	10a30	1 15	3 50	6 55
Greenock (Princes Pier)	...	arrive	8 35	10 55	1 30	4 5	7 10

			a.m.	a.m.	p.m.	p.m.	
Greenock (Princes Pier)	...	leave	8 40	11 5	1 35	4 20	...
Craigendoran	...	arrive	8 55	11 20	1 50	4 35	...
Do.	...	leave	9 0	11 26	2 5	4 38	...
Helensburgh	...	,,	9 7	11 36	2 15	4 47	...
Rosneath ...	...	,,	9 18	11 50	2 30	5 0	...
Clynder ...	...	,,	9 27	12 0	2 40	5 10	...
Rahane Ferry	...	,,	...	12 10	...	5 20	...
Mambeg ...	...	,,	...	12 15	...	5 25	...
Garelochhead	...	arrive	...	12 20	2 55	5 30	...

a Calls Helensburgh 10-37 a.m.

* Passengers join Steamer on outward run at time shown

LONDON & NORTH EASTERN RAILWAY

March 1932   (2½-M)   (S.C. 3172)

HUGH PATON & SONS, LTD., Printers, Edinburgh.

Lucy Ashton's Gareloch timetables for spring 1932, augmented by extra sailings on local Greenock holidays. *(CRSCA)*

In 1936, the LNER adopted a new livery with a grey hull and white upperworks and saloons. *Lucy Ashton* in seen in this livery in September 1936.

Lucy Ashton, again in the 1936-1939 period, with grey hull.

Lucy Ashton off Greenock with grey hull.

Lucy Ashton was the last Clyde steamer to have her bridge behind the funnel.

During the Second World War, Lucy Ashton maintained the LNER's services alone, serving both the Gareloch and Dunoon services. She is seen here in wartime grey in a photo dated 1940.

During the Second World War, another *Fair Maid* appeared at Craigendoran. This was a Forth steamer which was in use as a tender. From 21 to 30 March 1944 she stood in for *Lucy Ashton*, which had a damaged paddle float. *Fair Maid* had been built as the Clyde steamer *Madge Wildfire* in 1896 for Captain Bob Campbell's Kilmun to Glasgow run, coming under Caledonian Steam Packet ownership from 1889 to 1911, when she was sold to Captain Cameron. In 1913 she went to Buchanan Steamers Ltd as the *Isle of Skye*, and in 1927 to the Grangemouth and Forth Towing Co. as *Fair Maid*. She is seen here with flags flying for VE Day, 8 May 1945. The following year she was scrapped at Troon.

During the war, *Lucy Ashton* was fitted with a concrete wheelhouse, and towards the end of the war a wooden wheelhouse was fitted. After the war *Lucy* and the remainder of the fleet regained the traditional NB colours rather than the grey colour scheme of 1936-1939. She is seen here in 1947 at Craigendoran with the then new *Waverley*.

Lucy Ashton was painted in BR colours with a buff black-topped funnel in 1948, but survived only just over a year, before being laid up in Bowling Harbour in February 1949. *(DB)*

In January 1950 she was sold to the British Shipbuilding Research Association. Her accommodation, machinery and paddle boxes were stripped and she was fitted with two jet engines. The hull was used to test water resistance and laminar flow. In 1951 her hull was finally scrapped at the age of sixty-three.

A view of Craigendoran on 5 July 1919. The fan-boards show, to the left, *Dandie Dinmont* for Kilcreggan, Kirn, Dunoon, Innellan and Rothesay, a service that had only re-started on 1 May of that year after the war, and to the right, *Lucy Ashton* for the Gareloch. The steamer furthest left is the *Kenilworth*, as *Talisman* did not return from war service until October 1919 and *Waverley* and *Marmion* until 1920.

S.S. "Chancellor," Loch Long   Valentines Series

In 1888 the Loch Lomond Steamboat Company was taken over by the NBR with its four steamers. *Chancellor* of 1880, which was owned by the Lochlong and Loch Lomond Steamboat Co. and operated from Greenock to Arrochar via Craigendoran, was not included in the purchase, ownership being transferred to the Lochgoil and Lochlong Steamboat Co. *Chancellor* was the second Clyde steamer to be built in steel, the first having been the short-lived *Windsor Castle* of 1859.

In 1891 *Chancellor* was purchased by the Glasgow and South Western Railway and gave up the Craigendoran calls. She had previously almost been regarded as part of the Craigendoran fleet, and her sailings had appeared in the NB timetable. She is seen here in GSWR colours.

Four

The two *Ladies*

The *Lady Rowena* was built in 1891 to replace *Chancellor* on the Arrochar service, which vessel had been sold to the rival GSWR earlier that year. She was built by S. McKnight & Co. of Ayr, and was the first vessel in the fleet to have a full-width fore saloon, but retained single-cylinder machinery, again by Hutson & Corbett.

A postcard view of *Lady Rowena* at Arrochar. Passengers could walk to Tarbet pier on Loch Lomond and take the Loch Lomond steamer down to Balloch, a trip known as the 'Three Lochs Tour'.

Another postcard view of Arrochar, this time with two unidentified paddle steamers lying at the pier, the NB one, probably *Lady Rowena*, is to the right.

In 1903 *Lady Rowena* was sold to Bay of Naples owners, and came back to the UK to Newhaven under the ownership of R.R. Collard in 1908. In late 1911 she returned to the Clyde under the ownership of A.W. Cameron, and is seen here being tendered by the ferry at Mambeg, on the Gareloch, in this period. In 1912 she was chartered to Belfast Lough and after war service was sold to owners at Goole, Swansea, and Brighton respectively, until she was finally scrapped in 1922.

Another view of *Lady Rowena*, clearly showing the full-width fore saloon.

The second new steamer of 1891 was *Lady Clare*, which came from the yard of J.M. McArthur in Paisley with machinery by Hutson & Corbett. She was of a similar design to *Lucy Ashton*, and was intended to replace *Gareloch* on the Gareloch service.

A postcard view of *Lady Clare* at Garelochhead.

Five
Redgauntlet & Dandie

In 1895 Barclay Curle built *Redgauntlet*. With a length of 215ft and a gross tonnage of 227, she was the largest NB steamer so far. She was intended for the Rothesay route, but in 1898, after *Kenilworth* arrived, she was transferred to excursion work.

Redgauntlet seen with *Lady Clare* berthed outside her at Craigendoran. *Lady Clare* was sold in 1906 for use on Lough Foyle from Londonderry to Moville, and tendered to transatlantic liners calling at Lough Foyle. She saw little use after the First World War, when she had been used as a minesweeper, and after a spell laid up was broken up at Dumbarton in 1928.

In 1899 *Redgauntlet* was placed on longer excursion sailings to Brodick, Lamlash, Ayr and round Arran. While on one of the latter trips on 14 August, she ran aground on the Iron Rocks, off the south of Arran. She got off and the master beached her. *Waverley* was sent to bring her passengers home, and returned up-Firth from Whiting Bay with eleven passengers. The following morning *Lucy Ashton* was sent to Whiting Bay, from where she returned in the afternoon with the remaining passengers who had sepnt the night in hotels and boarding houses. *Redgauntlet* was finally refloated on 24 August and taken upriver for repairs.

In 1909 *Redgauntlet* was transferred to the Galloway Saloon Steam Packet Co. for service in the Firth of Forth. Her bows were altered to enable disembarkation at the Isle of May, where she is seen here. Following war service, she was sold to a French company based at Oran in Algeria, where she served without change of name until she was broken up in 1934.

Dandie Dinmont came from A. & J. Inglis in 1895, and was used on the Dunoon and Holy Loch run. She is seen here in her first season. She was lengthened in 1912.

A well-filled *Dandie Dinmont*, probably arriving at Dunoon.

Dandie Dinmont survived into LNER days, being laid up in 1926 and transferred to Hull to the New Holland ferry service in 1938, where her fore-saloon was removed to enable her to carry cars and she was renamed *Frodingham*. She was broken up at Ghent in January 1936. *(IQ)*

Six
Talisman & Kenilworth

The S. S. Talisman.

Talisman was built in 1896 by A. & J. Inglis for the Rothesay service. As built, she had her bridge aft of the funnel and a small fore saloon with alleyways round it. *(DB)*

In 1920, after returning from war service, *Talisman's* bridge was placed forward of the funnel, as in this illustration, and she received a larger full-width fore saloon.

A fore-quarter view of *Talisman* arriving at Dunoon, showing the open bridge forward of the funnel. *Talisman* was withdrawn after the 1934 summer season and scrapped by T.W. Ward at Barrow.

HIGHLAND MARY'S STATUE & PIER DUNOON

A pre-1914 postcard showing *Talisman* berthed at Dunoon pier with Highland Mary's statue in the foreground.

In 1898 *Kenilworth*, a sister of *Talisman*, was launched by A. & J. Inglis. She is seen here in pre-First World War condition with the bridge aft of the funnel. She was rather an anachronism, being fitted with a single-cylinder diagonal engine when the other railway companies had long since changed to compound machinery.

P. S. Kenilworth (1898) North British Railway Company Ltd.

Kenilworth in another pre-1914 view. The narrow fore saloon, which was replaced by a full-width one in 1919, can be clearly seen here. *Kenilworth* partnered *Talisman* on the Craigendoran-Rothesay service at this time.

"KENILWORTH".

Adamson, Rothesay

Kenilworth was altered, similarly to *Talisman*, when she came back from war service in 1919, and survived into the LNER grey hull phase from 1936 onwards.

Another photograph of *Kenilworth* with grey hull. By this time she was one of the last Clyde steamers with a single crank engine.

Kenilworth in 1936 with grey hull, and the CSP's *Duchess of Fife* in the background.

Kenilworth ended her days in 1938, when she was broken up in the yard she was built in.

Rothesay Pier prior to 1910, with *Kenilworth* nearest the camera, MacBrayne's *Columba* about to berth and a CSP paddle steamer across the far end of the pier.

Seven
Waverley of 1899

In 1899, a year after *Kenilworth* was built, *Waverley (I)* came into service. Also built by A. & J. Inglis, she had compound machinery, and a full-width fore saloon that extended forward of the mast. This early photograph of her shows the GSWR's *Viceroy* in the background, on the left.

Waverley leaving Craigmore. Craigmore Pier was situated at the entrance to Rothesay Bay, and was closed with the advent of the Second World War, although the pier house survives to this day as a café. *Waverley* was used on the round Bute cruise, replacing *Redgauntlet* which had introduced that service the previous summer, and went on to a variety of longer all-day sailings.

Dunoon pier in a postcard postmarked 1912, with *Waverley* to the left and *Talisman* to the right. Note the early cars in the view, along with the horse-drawn carriages awaiting the steamer passengers.

☞ **Begins on 8th June and ceases after 5th September.** ☜

～ DAILY ～
POPULAR EXCURSION
THROUGH THE
KYLES OF BUTE
AND ROUND
THE ISLAND OF BUTE,
Via CRAIGENDORAN.

	1st Class and Cabin. s. d.	3rd Class and Cabin. s. d.	3rd Class and Steerage. s. d.		1st Class and Cabin. s. d.	3rd Class and Cabin. s. d.	3rd Class and Steerage s. d.
Aberdeen	43 9	25 6	24 9	Hawick	27 9	17 3	16 6
Airdrie (South)	7 9	5 9	5 0	Hamilton	7 6	5 9	5 0
Alexandria	5 0	4 0	3 6	Helensburgh	2 8	...	2 0
Ardlui	6 6	5 11	5 5				
Arrochar & Tarbet	6 6	5 2	4 8	Innellan	2 6	...	2 0
				Jordanhill	5 6	4 6	3 9
Balloch	5 6	4 3	3 9				
Bathgate (Upper)	11 6	8 5	7 8	Kilcreggan	2 6	...	2 0
Berwick	29 0	18 1	17 4	Kirkcaldy	17 0	10 6	9 9
Bothwell	7 2	5 8	4 11	Kirn	2 6	...	2 0
Burnbank	7 6	5 9	5 0				
				Linlithgow	13 0	8 2	7 5
Clydebank (Central)	5 6	4 4	3 9				
Coatbridge (Central and Sunnyside)	7 6	5 6	4 9	Melrose	23 6	14 8	13 11
†Craigendoran	2 6		2 0				
Crianlarich	9 2	7 8	7 2	North Berwick	18 6	12 3	11 6
				Perth	21 3	13 2	12 5
Dalmuir	5 6	4 4	3 9	Polmont	11 0	7 4	6 7
Dalreoch	4 5	3 9	3 2				
Dumbarton	4 5	3 9	3 2	Renton	4 9	3 11	3 5
Dunbar	21 3	13 4	12 7	Rothesay	1 6	...	1 0
Dundee (Tay Bridge)	26 6	16 0	15 3	Row	3 6	3 1	2 7
Dunfermline (Upper and Lower)	16 8	10 8	9 11				
Dunoon	2 6	...	2 0	St Andrews	25 0	14 11	14 2
				Scotstounhill	5 6	4 6	3 9
Edinburgh (Waverley & Haymarket)	13 0	8 6	7 9	Shandon	4 2	3 6	3 0
Edinburgh Suburban Stations and Stns. on Leith & Granton Branches	13 3	8 8	7 11	Singer	5 6	4 4	3 9
				Tighnabruaich	1 6	...	...
Falkirk (Grahamston and High)	11 0	7 4	6 7				
Fort-William	26 6	16 1	15 7	Uddingston and Uddingston West	7 2	5 6	4 9
Galashiels	22 6	14 1	13 4	Victoria Park, Whiteinch	5 6	4 6	3 9
Glasgow (Queen Street) and City and District Stations	5 6	4 6	3 9	Yoker	5 6	4 4	3 9

TICKETS VALID FOR THE SEASON.

† The Tickets from Craigendoran Pier are issued on board the Steamer.

Advertisement in the 1914 NB Tourist Programme for *Waverley*'s Round Bute cruises with a list of fares from various North British stations.

Waverley arriving at Helensburgh pier in a pre-1914 postcard view.

Waverley served in the First World War as a minesweeper from November 1915 until April 1919. *(GEL)*

When in naval use during the First World War *Waverley* had her promenade deck extended to the bow, and this feature was retained when she re-entered peace-time service in 1920. She is seen here at Lochgoilhead, on the Arrochar service, which she maintained from 1920 until her withdrawal after the 1938 season.

Waverley in her 1920-1932 condition.

NORTH BRITISH RAILWAY COMPANY.

EVENING CRUISES

BY SALOON STEAMER

"WAVERLEY"

(Weather Permitting).

Wednesday,	2nd August,	-	To	LARGS BAY
Tuesday,	8th ,,	-	,,	LOCH LONG
Wednesday,	16th ,,	-	,,	LOCH STRIVEN
Tuesday,	22nd ,,	-	,,	CUMBRAE
Wednesday,	30th ,,	-	,,	LOCH GOIL

TRAIN AND STEAMER HOURS.

TRAIN	Going		Returning		FARES
	P. M.		P. M.		Third Class and Steamer
QUEEN STREET, - - -	6	5	10	59	
CHARING CROSS, - - -	5	34	10	56	
PARTICK, - - - -	6	13	10	52	3/6
CLYDEBANK (Central), A -	6	22	10	36	
DALMUIR, - - - -	6	0	10	32	
DUMBARTON, - - -	6	34	10	16	2/9
CARDROSS, - - - -	6	42	10	6	2/6
STEAMER					Steamer Fare
CRAIGENDORAN PIER, -	6	55	9	50	
HELENSBURGH, - -	7	10	9	55	2/-
KILCREGGAN, - - -	7	25	9	35	Children above 3 and under 12 years of age half-fare.

NOTE.—A Passengers from Clydebank are Conveyed to Singer on return.

A handbill for a series of evening cruises by the *Waverley* in August 1922. Evening cruises were very popular on the Clyde in the inter-war years and were offered by all the main operators. *(CRSCA)*

Another view of *Waverley* in her 1920-1932 condition.

An unusual view of *Waverley* and MacBrayne's *Iona* at Arrochar. In the summers of 1928 and 1929, *Iona* was placed on MacBrayne's Lochgoilhead mail run, which was extended to Arrochar.

Waverley during her winter lay-up in Bowling harbour. Alongside her is MacBrayne's *Iona*, and behind her *Eagle III*, *Dandie Dinmont* and two other unidentified paddle steamers.

Another view of *Waverley* during her winter lay-up, with *Columba* and *Fusilier* alongside and at least five more steamers aft of her.

In 1936, *Waverley*, like the remainder of the LNER fleet, adopted the new colours of grey hull and white saloons. In 1933, she had been refitted to match the comfort of the then new *Jeanie Deans*, and like the *Jeanie* had received new deck saloons, as seen in this picture.

A bow three-quarter view of *Waverley* in grey hull condition.

Waverley was laid up for the 1939 season in Bowling before being requisitioned by the Admiralty and converted to a minesweeper at Inglis' yard. On 29 May 1940, when in use at the Dunkirk evacuation, she was bombed and sank with heavy loss of life.

Waverley berthed at Rothesay. *Jupiter*, in GSWR colours, has just left the pier.

Eight
Marmion

Marmion was the final NB steamer, built by A. & J. Inglis in 1906 for the Loch Long and Arrochar service.

Marmion in original condition at Lochgoilhead.

Marmion served as a minesweeper during the First World War, from June 1915 until April 1919. *(GEL)*

Marmion was plated to the bow during her First World War service, and this feature was retained when she resumed Clyde service in June 1920. The extra weight forward affected her trim, as seen in this photograph. *(GEL)*

After the First World War, *Marmion* was given a promenade deck built up to the bow, like *Waverley*. Her speed dropped from 19 to 14 knots and she became very unstable. As a result she was withdrawn after the 1920 season. She was altered in 1923, with the built-up bow being removed and the saloon front moved back well behind the funnel, to give her a much smaller fore saloon than she had originally had. She did not re-enter service until 1926, replacing *Dandie Dinmont* after the latter had gone to the Humber.

Marmion was re-boilered in 1932 and given a new funnel. At the same time her aft saloon was converted to a tea-bar and the sills of the windows were lowered considerably, as seen in this photograph.

A stern three-quarter view of *Marmion* in 1932-1935 condition.

A post-war view of Rothesay with *Marmion* at the pier.

Another view of Rothesay and *Marmion*. By this time, she was on the Craigendoran-Rothesay service with an afternoon trip to the Kyles of Bute piers.

Afternoon Excursion

TO THE

KYLES OF BUTE

BY STEAMER

"MARMION"

OR OTHER STEAMER

Daily Except Saturdays

FROM 12TH JULY TO 11TH SEPTEMBER

From		Going.	Returning.	Return Fares.	
				Cabin	Steerage
		p.m.	p.m.	S. D.	S. D.
Helensburgh* ...	...	depart 12 15	arrive 7†12		
Craigendoran ...	...	,, 12 32	,, 6 40	3 9	3 0
Kilcreggan	... ...	,, 12 48	,, 6 20		
Kirn ...	... ...	,, 1 3	...		
Dunoon	... ...	,, 1 10	,, 6 0	3 0	2 3
Innellan	... ...	,, 1 30	,, 5 40		
Craigmore	... ...	,, 1 50	,, 5 20		
Rothesay	... ...	,, 2 15	,, 5 5	1 6	1 0
Tighnabruaich	...	arrive 2 55	depart 4 15	...	...
Kames ...	... ...	,, 3 0	,, 4 10	...	...

* Steamer may not call at Helensburgh at low tide.

† Not during September.

Passengers have over an hour ashore at Tighnabruaich or Kames.

July 1926   (15-M)   S.C. 2469

A 1926 handbill for Kyles of Bute cruises on *Marmion*. (CRSCA)

Marmion in grey hull condition.

Marmion at speed with grey hull, 1936-1939.

In 1936 evening cruises from Rothesay to view the illuminations from Rothesay Bay were offered by *Marmion*. (*CRSCA*)

Marmion at Arrochar in 1938. This was an unusual call, as she was normally on the Rothesay service in that year.

In September 1939, the Admiralty again requisitioned *Marmion*. Her bow was again built up as it had been in the First World War. She was based with the 12th Minesweeping Flotilla at Harwich and made three successful trips to Dunkirk.

Marmion was sunk by German aircraft while at anchor off Harwich on the night of April 8 1941. Although raised she was beyond reconditioning and was scrapped. *(GEL)*

Nine
Fair Maid, chartered ships and others

In 1915 the NBR, presumably believing that the war would be over by Christmas, ordered another paddle steamer from A. & J. Inglis. She was named *Fair Maid*, but was taken over by the Admiralty in December 1915, and sunk by a mine on 6 November 1916 in the North Sea. She is seen here on trials in the Gareloch in February 1916.

LONDON AND NORTH EASTERN RAILWAY

Conveyance of Goods Traffic

to and from

Clyde Watering Places

The Company hereby gives notice that the following arrangements are in operation in respect of Traffic to and from Clyde Watering Places by their Steamers :—

1.—That no Package which exceeds 3 cwts. in weight will be accepted for conveyance by the Company's Steamers, excepting Wines, Spirits, Beer, &c., in Barrels.

2.—That Cement and Artificial Manures in consignments exceeding 10 cwts. in weight will not be accepted for conveyance by the Company's Steamers.

3.—That Coal and Lime Traffic will not be accepted for conveyance by the Company's Steamers.

4.—That the Company reserves the right to refuse to carry Cargo by any Steamer and on any day.

LONDON AND NORTH EASTERN RAILWAY

Train and Steamboat Services

TO AND FROM THE

CLYDE COAST

Via **Craigendoran**

| 1923 | :: | MAY | :: | 1923 |

The L. & N. E. Railway Company reserve the right to alter any of the Sailings herein detailed, if necessary or to cancel them in whole or in part

R. L. WEDGWOOD
Chief General Manager

(3½·M)

HUGH PATON & SONS, LTD., PRINTERS, EDINBURGH.

The cover of the May 1923 LNER Clyde Coast timetable.

To the Clyde Coast

MAY 1923

Train		a.m.		a.m.	a.m.
nburgh (Waverley) ... leave		6 25		...	9 5
drie (South) ... ... ,,		7 9		...	9 27
tbridge (Sunnyside) ... ,,		7 15		...	9 34
milton ... ... ,,		6 58		...	9 40
sgow { Bridgeton Cross ,,		7 36		10 3	10 21
High Street ... ,,		7 40		10 7	10 25
Queen Street ... ,,		7 55		10 23	10 35
Charing Cross ... ,,		7 58		...	10 38
Partick ... ... ,,		8 4		10 32	10 44
debank (Central) ... ,,		...		...	...
ger ... ... ,,		8.16		10 48	...
muir ... ... ,,		...		...	10 55
nbarton		8 28		10 57	11 6

Steamer

igendoran ... ... leave	8 55		9 0	9 0	11 35	11 35	11 35	11 45
ensburgh ¶ ... arrive	...		9 7	9 7			11 42	11 52
eneath ... ... ,,	...		9 20	9 20			11 55	12 5
nder ... ... ,,	...		9 30	9 30			12 5	12 15
ane Ferry ... ,,	...		9 40				12 15	12 25
mbeg ... ... ,,	...						12 20	12 30
elochhead ... ,,	...						12 25	12 35
reggan ... ... ,,	9 10				11 50	11 50		
nter's Quay ... ,,	...					12 27		
one ... ... ,,	...					12 32		
mun ... ... ,,	...					12 39		
nadam ... ... ,,	...					12 46		
n ... ... ,,	...				12 5	12 20		
ıoon ... ... ,,	9 30		9 45		12 15	12 10		
ellan ... ... ,,	...		9 55		12 35	...		
gmore ... ... ,,	...		...		12 55	...		
hesay ... ... ,,	...		10 15		1 0	...		

(Column notes: MacBrayne's Steamer · Except Saturdays. · Saturdays only. · Except Saturdays · Saturdays only. · Saturdays only. · Except Saturdays.)

Steamers may leave Craigendoran five minutes earlier if trains in connection have arrived.

¶ Steamers may not call at Helensburgh Pier at Low Tide.

2

To the Clyde Coast

MAY 1923

Train		Sats. only. p.m.	Sats. only. a.m. 10 35 p.m.	Ex. Sats. p.m. 2 0	Sats. only. p.m. 2 0	Ex. Sats. p.m.	p.m. 4 0
Edinburgh (Waverley) ... leave		...	12 7	3 8	3 8	4 5	5 12
Airdrie (South) ... ,,		...	12 14	3 14	3 14	4 11	5 18
Coatbridge (Sunnyside) ... ,,		...	12 13	3 18	3 18	...	4 43
Hamilton ... ... ,,		12 42	12 57	3A44	3 55	4 51	5 46
Glasgow { Bridgeton Cross ,,		12 46	1 1	3A48	4 1	4 55	5 50
High reet ... ,,		1 5	1 10	4A0	4 20	5 8	6 5
Queen Street ... ,,		..	1 14	3 13	4 23	4 23	...
Charing Cross ... ,,		1 13		3 19	4 29	4 29	6 13
Partick ... ... ,,		...	...	...	...	...	6 22
Clydebank (Central) ... ,,		...	1 29	3 35	4 45	4 45	5 56
Singer ... ... ,,		...	1 33	3 39	4 48	4 48	6 0
Dalmuir ... ... ,,		1 34	...	4 26	5 4	5 4	6 34
Dumbarton ... ... ,,							

Steamer

Craigendoran ... leave	2 5	2 10	4 45	5 40	5 40	5 50	6 55	7 10
Helensburgh ¶ ... arrive	2 12				5 47	5 57	
Roseneath ... ... ,,	2 25				6 0	6 10	
Clynder ... ... ,,	2 35				6 10	6 20	
Rahane Ferry ... ,,	2 45				6 20	6 30	
Mambeg ... ... ,,	2 50				6 25	6 35	
Garelochhead ... ,,	2 55				6 30	6 40	
Kilcreggan		2 25	5 0	5 55			7 10	7 25
Hunter's Quay ... ,,		...	5 20				7 40	7 55
Strone ... ... ,,		...	5 15				7 45	8 0
Kilmun ... ... ,,		...					7 52	8 7
Ardnadam ... ... ,,		...					8 0	8 15
Kirn ... ... ,,		2 40	5 25				7 35	7 50
Dunoon ... ... ,,		2 45	5 30	6 15			7 30	7 45
Innellan ... ... ,,		3 5					
Craigmore ... ... ,,		3 25					
Rothesay ... ... ,,		3 30					

(Column notes: Except Saturdays. · Saturdays only.)

Steamers may leave Craigendoran five minutes earlier if trains in connection have arrived.

A.—No luggage.

¶ Steamers may not call at Helensburgh Pier at Low Tide.

3

Inside pages of the May 1923 LNER Clyde Coast timetable.

In 1917, the NBR had only *Dandie Dinmont* and *Lucy Ashton* in service, and when *Lucy Ashton* was off service for ten months from June, MacBrayne's *Fusilier* (1888) was chartered for around ten days for the Gareloch service. She is seen here in a more peaceful era, at anchor off Staffa on 13 July 1929.

Fusilier was replaced by *Isle of Cumbrae*, ex-*Jeanie Deans (I)*, and from the end of September until May 1918 MacBrayne's *Mountaineer* (1910) was chartered, initially to replace *Lucy Ashton* and then to allow *Dandie Dinmont* a much-needed overhaul.

Ten
The second *Jeanie*

A fake view of Craigendoran pier in the early thirties. The image of *Jeanie Deans* lying off has been inserted in the photo for publicity purposes. From left to right we see *Marmion*, *Kenilworth*, *Talisman*, and *Lucy Ashton*. Note the fan boards announcing *Talisman* for Kilcreggan, Kirn, Dunoon, Innellan and Rothesay.

In 1931, the LNER took delivery of *Jeanie Deans*, possibly the ultimate Clyde paddle steamer. Built to compete with the CSP's *Duchess of Montrose*, which had appeared the previous year, she came from the Fairfield yard and had the first set of triple-expansion engines built for a Clyde steamer. She is seen here as she first appeared, with two funnels of equal height.

Another shot of *Jeanie Deans*, in her first season, with a full load of passengers.

EVENING CRUISE

By NEW STEAMER

"JEANIE DEANS"

(Weather Permitting)

Round CUMBRAE

THURSDAY, 28th MAY

TRAIN AND STEAMER HOURS.

TRAIN.	Going.	Return- ing.	FARES.	
	p.m.	p.m.	First Class & Steamer.	Third Class & Steamer.
			S. D.	S. D.
Bridgeton Cross ...	6 28	11 19	4 4	3 3
Queen Street	6 35	11 14		
Partick	6 43	11 7		
Anniesland for Knightswood ...	6 48	11 2		
Clydebank (Central)*	6 22	10 53		
Dumbarton	6 34	10 41	3 1	2 6
Cardross	6 41	10 33	2 3	2 0
			STEAMER FARE.	
Steamer—			S. D.	
Craigendoran Pier...	7 20	10 20	1 9	
Helensburgh ...	7 30	10 30		

*Clydebank passengers are conveyed to Singer Station on return journey.

NOTE—Parties of not less than 50 Third Class Passengers from Glasgow will be conveyed at Reduced Fare of 3s. by previous arrangement with the District Superintendent, Queen Street Station, Glasgow.

MUSIC ON BOARD

LONDON & NORTH EASTERN RAILWAY

May 1931.   (10-M)   (S.C, 1529.)

HUGH PATON & SONS, LTD,, Printers, Edinburgh.

A 1931 handbill for an evening cruise on the new *Jeanie Deans* round Cumbrae. *Jeanie Deans* had run trials on 7 May 1931, and this may have been her first public sailing. (CRSCA)

ROTHESAY ILLUMINATIONS

EVENING CRUISE

By New Steamer "JEANIE DEANS"
(Weather Permitting)

TO

LOCH STRIVEN

AND

ROTHESAY BAY

ON

Friday, 28th August 1931

TRAIN AND STEAMER HOURS

FROM	GOING	RETURNING	FARES			
			1st Class		3rd Class	
	p.m.	p.m.	S. D.		S. D.	
Bridgeton Cross ...	6 46	12 7	4	4	3	3
Queen Street ...	6 53	12 2	4	4	3	3
Charing Cross ...	6 56	11 59	4	4	3	3
Partick	7 2	11 54	4	4	3	3
Anniesland ...	7 7	11 49	4	4	3	3
Singer	7 15	11 41	4	4	3	3
Dalmuir	7 18	11 38	4	4	3	3
Kilpatrick	7 20	11 34	4	1	3	1
Balloch	6 58	11 53	3	11	3	0
Alexandria ...	7 3	11 49	3	7	2	10
Renton	7 7	11 45	3	5	2	8
Dumbarton ...	7 19	11 34	3	1	2	6
Cardross	7 26	11 27	2	3	2	0
			Steamer Fare			
Craigendoran ...	7 45	11 5	1 9			

NOTE—Parties of not less than 50 Third Class Passengers from Glasgow will be conveyed at Reduced Fare of 3s. by previous arrangement with the District Superintendent, Queen Street Station, Glasgow.

MUSIC ON BOARD

LONDON & NORTH EASTERN RAILWAY

August 1931.   (10-M)   (S.C. 2305)

HUGH PATON & SONS, LTD., Printers, Edinburgh.

Rothesay Illuminations, at the end of August, were a favourite venue for evening cruises. In 1931 *Jeanie Deans* offered a rail connected cruise from Craigendoran. *(CRSCA)*

In her first season, *Jeanie Deans* operated to Lochgoilhead and Arrochar. She is seen here at Lochgoilhead with MacBrayne's Lochgoilhead mail vessel, the motor launch *Comet*.

For the 1932 season, a steel observation lounge was fitted forward on the promenade deck, and her funnels heightened to avoid smuts dropping on passengers on the after deck. The fore funnel was heightened more than the aft one, giving the steamer an unbalanced appearance.

In 1932 *Jeanie Deans* was placed on a variety of longer excursions, on Tuesdays and Thursdays, to Ayr and around Ailsa Craig. She is seen here leaving Ayr in that season.

She continued her Arrochar sailings on Mondays, and is seen here with the Caledonian Steam Packet's Ayr excursion steamer *Duchess of Hamilton* at that pier.

A shot of *Jeanie Deans* in her 1932 to 1935 condition at Lochgoilhead Pier.

Jeanie Deans at Arrochar in her grey hull state. In 1938, after the withdrawal of *Kenilworth*, the long-distance cruises were withdrawn and she operated mainly on the Arrochar run.

HELLO, ENGLAND!!

The CLYDE COAST TOURING & ENTERTAINMENT BUREAU

PRESENT AN

ANGLO-SCOTTISH

RADIO CRUISE

WITH

PERSONAL APPEARANCE OF

IAN MACLEAN, Variety Artist,

... TO ...

GARELOCHHEAD

On *MONDAY, 16th AUGUST,*

BY THE

RADIO EQUIPPED JEANIE DEANS

The Ship with the Most Famous Dancing Deck and specially-constructed Studio for relaying First-Class Entertainment to **EVERY PART OF THE SHIP.**

COME AND HEAR THIS FIRST-CLASS ARTIST

PROGRAMME OF—

SCOTTISH AND ENGLISH TRADITIONAL SONGS

DANCING on the FAMOUS "QUARTER DECK"

(Eightsome Reels, Old-Fashioned Dancing, Modern Dancing, Paul Jones, etc.)

COMMUNITY SINGING, led by *The Clyde Singer*

WE ALSO HAVE A NOVELTY HUNT

Twenty Novelty People to be found to Win a Prize.

LEAVING—

ROTHESAY 6-30, LARGS 7, DUNOON 7-45 P.M.

FARE, - - 2s. Children Half-Fare

TICKETS ON BOARD, or at Pierheads, or L.N.E.R. Office, Rothesay.

ROTHESAY EXPRESS

A handbill for a radio cruise to Garelochhead aboard *Jeanie Deans*, a vessel described as 'The Ship with the Most Famous Dancing Deck', in 1937. On the same evening, *Waverley* was on a cruise from Craigendoran to Brodick. (CRSCA)

In 1936 *Jeanie Deans*, along with the other LNER paddlers, was given the new grey colour scheme.

The aft deck shelter, which in pre-war years did not have a passenger deck and lifeboats on top, can be seen in this postcard, posted in 1938.

In September 1939, *Jeanie Deans* was taken up for war service as a minesweeper. She was the flagship of the 11th Minesweeping Flotilla, based initially on the Clyde, and later at Portsmouth and Milford Haven. In March 1941 she was moved to the Thames and fitted out as an auxiliary anti-aircraft vessel. As seen in this photo, a concrete wheelhouse was fitted and the observation saloon removed.

Jeanie Deans, still in wartime camouflage colours, in dry dock.

BOWLING HARBOUR, RIVER CLYDE

In 1948, with the nationalization of the railways, the LNER steamers adopted the CSP colours of buff black-topped funnel and white deck saloons. This postcard of Bowling Harbour shows *Jeanie Deans* to the right, still in LNER colours, *Waverley* to the left, in BR colours, and a Blue Star Line ship outward bound down the river.

In 1946 *Jeanie Deans* returned to Clyde service, with a black hull, new funnels of equal height, a wooden wheelhouse and dining saloon windows in brown to match the saloons and ventilators. *(AB)*

83

In the early part of the BR era, *Jeanie Deans* had her dining saloon windows painted brown. A weekday afternoon around Bute had been introduced in 1953 and this remained her preserve until withdrawal. The other change in BR days was to insert calls at Gourock in most Craigendoran to Dunoon sailings.

JEANIE DEANS, AT ROTHESAY PIER

A view of *Jeanie Deans* at Rothesay Pier in the late fifties or early sixties.

CLYDE STEAMER, P.S. "JEANIE DEANS"

PHOTO
SCOTTISH SUNDAY
EXPRESS

B 9779

An aerial view of *Jeanie Deans* in the same period, showing the new position of the aft lifeboats and passenger deck above the after deck shelter.

A magnificent view of *Jeanie Deans* between Craigendoran and Dunoon on 15 July 1961. The funnel rings where she had previously worn the white ring of the LNER livery can be seen in this picture.

Jeanie Deans passing Toward lighthouse, inward bound for Rothesay in around 1964.

Jeanie Deans at the end of her Clyde career. At this stage she was alternating weekly with *Waverley*, doing an afternoon around Bute cruise from Monday to Friday, a Tighnabruiach cruise on Saturday, and a Sunday cruise to Skipness.

Jeanie Deans (right) and *Waverley* lying in the Albert Harbour in the 1964-1965 winter. *Jeanie Deans* had made her last Clyde sailing on 28 September 1964.

Waverley, with *Jeanie Deans* beside her, lying in Greenock's Albert Harbour in the 1964-1965 winter. Note the protective caps on *Jeanie's* funnels.

Following page: Jeanie Deans photographed from *Waverley* off Innellan in 1963. By the early sixties *Jeanie Deans* and *Waverley* swapped rosters weekly, with one steamer offering a morning return to Rothesay and an afternoon sailing to Rothesay and around Bute on Mondays to Fridays, to Tighnabruaich on Saturdays and a cruise round Bute and Cumbrae or to off Skipness on Sundays. The other steamer sailed to Arran via the Kyles of Bute on Mondays, to Lochgoilhead and Arrochar on Tuesdays and Thursdays, round the Lochs and Firth of Clyde on Wednesdays (this sailing combined a morning cruise round Bute anti-clockwise, with an afternoon cruise to off Carrick Castle), and from the Clyde Coast piers up-river to Glasgow on Fridays (although this sailing was sometimes undertaken by *Caledonia*). Saturdays were given over to a series of runs for Craigendoran to Rothesay. *(DD)*

In November 1965, *Jeanie Deans* was sold to the London-based Coastal Steam Packet Co. Ltd. She was repainted in LNER colours, renamed *Queen of the South* and attempted to make a career on the Thames for the next two summers, operating from Tower Pier to Southend-on-Sea. This is a John Nicholson painting used as an official card by her owners.

Queen of the South at Tower Pier in 1966. Breakdowns meant that a lot of scheduled sailings had to be cancelled in that year. Prior to the 1967 season her boiler was re-tubed, but boiler and paddle wheel problems again put paid to plans to operate her after only two and a half weeks of sailings. On 27 December 1967 she was towed to Belgium to be broken up at Boom, near Antwerp.

Eleven

Talisman,
the clockwork mouse

Talisman (II) was a revolutionary ship when built by A. & J. Inglis for the LNER in 1935. She
was the world's first diesel/electric passenger paddler, and the only such vessel ever to feature
direct drive to the paddles. In her first season, as seen here, she was in traditional LNER livery
with a black hull. Pre-war she had solid bulwarks, and in 1935 these were painted black.

Special Evening Cruises

(Weather permitting)

BY NEW DIESEL-ELECTRIC PADDLE VESSEL

"TALISMAN"

Wednesday, 10th July	**MILLPORT**
Thursday, 18th July	**ROTHESAY** (FOR ANNUAL FAIR)
Tuesday, 23rd July	**LARGS**

STEAMER TIMES

	Going	Returning
	p.m.	p.m.
*GARELOCHHEAD	5 35	11 30
*CLYNDER	5 50	11 15
*ROSNEATH	6 0	11 5
CRAIGENDORAN	6 50	10 50
HELENSBURGH	7 5	11 0
KILCREGGAN	7 20	10 35

* Gareloch passengers change Steamers at Craigendoran.

Passengers will have time ashore, and Steamer will leave on return journey at 9-30 p.m. prompt.

FARE 1/9

MUSIC ON BOARD

L·N·E·R

Hugh Paton & Sons, Ltd., Printers, Edinburgh   June 1935   (5-M)   (S.S. 5750)

A handbill for evening cruises by the new *Talisman* in July 1935, showing connecting services from Garelochhead. (*CRSCA*)

In 1935, *Talisman* appeared in the new LNER grey-hulled livery. Her service in this period was a morning run from Craigendoran to Rothesay, and an afternoon run to the Kyles of Bute, finishing at Auchenlochan.

L.N.E.R. DIESEL ELECTRIC PADDLE VESSEL, "TALISMAN."   A.40

A broadside view of *Talisman* in the condition she was in from 1936 to 1938.

The cover of the 1938 LNER summer steamer timetable, showing *Talisman*.

THE L·N·E·R CLYDE FLEET

operates from

CRAIGENDORAN

and consists

of

Diesel Electric Paddle Vessel "TALISMAN."

This ship was added to the fleet in 1935. Known as the "all-electric" ship, she is the largest Diesel Electric Paddle Vessel afloat, and the only one on the Firth of Clyde services. The direct control of her machinery from the bridge is one of the many novelties of her equipment. Modern electric lighting, hot and cold water, tastefully-furnished saloons, and all-weather deck shelters ensure that passengers shall enjoy a high standard of comfort on board. The absence of smoke and soot from the funnel is an often-appreciated feature of travel by the "Talisman."

Paddle Steamer "JEANIE DEANS."

The "Jeanie Deans," built in 1931, is the largest and fastest paddle ship on the Firth of Clyde. Provided with every modern convenience, including all-weather deck shelters, she has a wide and increasing reputation for smooth sailing and comfort. Passengers are sometimes puzzled to explain why one of this ship's funnels should be longer than the other. This has been arranged so that any smoke from the first funnel shall pass clear of the second, and the possibility of soot falling on the decks be avoided.

Paddle Steamer "WAVERLEY."

Certain of the Clyde steamers, by the proved quality of their service as well as by the excellence of their appointments, have won their way into the favour—one almost writes affection—of holiday-makers all over the country. It may truly be said that the "Waverley" is one of these. In 1933 she was fitted with all-weather deck shelters, which enable passengers to view the scenery under cover, and which are a modern development in Clyde steamer construction.

Paddle Steamer "MARMION."
Do.   "LUCY ASHTON."

All the L.N.E.R. Clyde vessels bear names made famous by the genius of Sir Walter Scott. The funnels are coloured Red with White band and Black top.

Real Photo Postcards of the ships are on sale on board and at L.N.E.R. Stations, Bookstalls and Offices.

16

Steward Department

BILL OF FARE

FIRST-CLASS SALOON	SECOND-CLASS SALOON
BREAKFAST ... ... **3s.** From 7-0 a.m. Porridge and Milk, Fish, Ham and Egg, Sausage, Cold Meats, Tea, Coffee, Toast and Preserves.	**BREAKFAST** ... ... **2s.** From 7-0 a.m. Porridge and Milk, Ham and Egg, Sausage, Tea, Coffee, Toast and Preserves.
BREAKFAST ... ... **2s. 6d.** Porridge and Milk. With Single Dish as above.	**BREAKFAST** ... ... Porridge and Milk. With Single Dish as above.
LUNCHEON ... ... **3s. 6d.** From 10-15 a.m. Soup, Fish, Cold Joints, Roast Beef, Lamb, Braised Ham, Ox Tongue, Pressed Beef, Vegetables and Potatoes, Sweets, Salad, Biscuits and Cheese.	**LUNCHEON** ... ... From 10-15 a.m. Soup, Fish, Cold Joints, Vegetables, Sweets or Biscuits and Cheese.
LUNCHEON ... ... **2s. 6d.** Soup, Cold Joints, Vegetables, Sweets or Biscuits and Cheese.	**LUNCHEON** ... ... **2s. 6d.** Soup, Cold Joints, Vegetables, Sweets, Biscuits and Cheese.
LUNCHEON ... ... **2s.** Cold Joints, Vegetables, with choice of Soup or Sweets.	**LUNCHEON** ... ... Cold Joints, Vegetables, with choice Soup or Sweets.
TEA ... ... **3s.** From 3-0 p.m. Fish, Cold Meats, Eggs (boiled or poached), Toast, Teabread, Biscuits and Preserves.	**TEA** ... ... **2s. 6d.** From 3-0 p.m. Fish, Cold Meats, Toast, Teabread, Biscuits and Preserves.
TEA ... ... **2s. 6d.** With Single Dish as above.	**TEA** ... ... With Single Dish as above.
TEA (Plain) ... ... **1s. 3d.** Toast, Teabread, Biscuits and Preserves.	**TEA (Plain)** ... ... **1s. 3d.** Toast, Teabread, Biscuits and Preserves.

SUNDRIES

(Served in Dining Saloons when accommodation is available)

Cold Joint and Vegetable	...	...	1s. 6d.
Soup, with Bread	...	...	6d.
Sandwiches	...	...	6d. and 1s.
Biscuits and Cheese	...	...	6d.
Cup of Tea or Coffee ...	...	...	3d.
Do.	with Biscuits	...	6d.

TEA ROOM

Tea, Coffee, Cakes, Biscuits, Teabread, etc., are served at any time in the Tea Room.

REFRESHMENTS, CONFECTIONS, Etc.

Wines, Spirits and Cigarettes are available in the Saloons and Smoke Rooms at moderate prices. Postcards, Camera Films, Ices and a selection of popular Confections are on sale at the shops on board.

17

From the 1938 timetable, a description of the steamers, and, on the opposite page, the Stewards Department bill of Fare.

Following page: In 1938 the fleet visited the Clyde, and a variety of cruises were offered to view the ships of HM Fleet. (CRSCA)

VISIT OF HOME FL

SPECIAL SHORT CRUISES
TO VIEW
SHIPS OF H.M. FLEET
ON
SUNDAYS
26th JUNE and 3rd JULY

Leaving CRAIGENDORAN 1-10 p.m.
Leaving HELENSBURGH 1-20 p.m.
and thereafter as required

H.M.S. "NELSON" will be open for inspection on 26th June, and H.M.S. "RODNEY" on 3rd July. If the Steamer is permitted alongside, passengers may go on board these battleships.

Fare 1/-

EVENING TRIPS ROUND FLEET
Leaving CRAIGENDORAN 6-35 and 7-5 p.m.
and HELENSBURGH 6-45 and 7-15 p.m.

Fare 1/-

Trains in connection from Glasgow (Queen Street and Partick), Clydebank and Dumbarton.

SPECIAL S
T
SHIPS O
(including B
"RODNEY" and
and Aircraft Carr

at Tai

SATURD
MONDA
TUESDA
THURS
FRIDAY,
SATURD

Leaving CRAIG
Leaving HELE

* 15 minute

Trains in connecti
Street), Partic
etc.

ET TO THE CLYDE

CRUISES	**SPECIAL EVENING EXCURSION**
~~v~~	**TO**
M. FLEET	**DUNOON**
"NELSON,"	
AL SOVEREIGN "	with opportunity of viewing
OURAGEOUS ")	**SHIPS OF H.M. FLEET**
Bank	(including Battleships "NELSON," "RODNEY" and "ROYAL SOVEREIGN" and Aircraft Carrier "COURAGEOUS")
th June	at Tail of the Bank
th ,,	**ON**
th ,,	**WEDNESDAY, 29th JUNE**
th ,,	
t July	
d ,,	

RAN 7*50 p.m.
GH 8*0 p.m.

		Outward	Return
CRAIGENDORAN	leave	7 48 arrive	10 0
HELENSBURGH	,,	7 55 ,,	10 7
DUNOON	... arrive	8 25 leave	9 20

n 2nd July.

Glasgow (Queen
bank, Dumbarton,

Fare 1/2

Craigendoran with *Lucy Ashton* lying off and *Talisman* berthed at the pier in the 1936-38 grey hull era.

In 1939 the grey on *Talisman's* hull was extended to the top of the saloon windows. In that season, only three vessels were in service, *Lucy Ashton* being spare and *Waverley* laid up. On 24 July *Talisman* had to be withdrawn after a series of cracks in the engine cylinder castings. She was laid up at Bowling alongside *Waverley*, and replaced by *Lucy Ashton* for the remainder of that foreshortened season.

In September 1939 the English Electric Company agreed to replace the engine cylinder castings that had cracked, and this work was done in May 1940. On 24 June 1940 she was requisitioned as HMS *Aristocrat*. She served as an anti-aircraft protection ship, took part in the D-Day landings as an HQ ship and was the first ship to enter Antwerp after the German withdrawal. Her full story can be read in the little book *HMS Aristocrat – A paddler at war* by Alan Brown and Richard Polglaze.

In 1946, *Talisman* returned to the Clyde. She gained a wheelhouse, her solid bulwarks were replaced by iron rails and she returned to her original livery of 1935. She is seen here leaving Rothesay with *Caledonia* at the pier.

Another view of Rothesay in 1946-1947 with *Talisman* and *Caledonia*. *Talisman* was on the Craigendoran to Rothesay service in that era, with only a Sunday afternoon jaunt to her old haunts of the Kyles of Bute.

DEISEL ELECTRIC PADDLE VESSEL TALISMAN   A.4031.

In 1948, with railway nationalization, *Talisman* became part of the British Railways fleet and got a buff black-topped funnel. Valentine's, anxious to be up to date, published this card, a view of *Talisman* in 1936-1938 hull colours with a funnel retouched to BR colours, a livery she never bore.

Up until 1951 the summer schedules for *Talisman* continued more or less as in LNER days. In summer 1952 she changed places with *Waverley* and worked the Lochgoilhead and Arrochar service. In summer 1953 she saw little service as *The Maid of Argyll* had come out and in March 1954 she received new diesel engines built by British Polar, replacing the old and troublesome English Electric ones.

DIESEL ELECTRIC PADDLE VESSEL, "TALISMAN"   B 9932

From 1954 until her withdrawal, *Talisman* served the Wemyss Bay-Largs-Millport (Old Pier) service, replacing *Marchioness of Lorne*.

In late 1955 *Talisman's* paddle boxes were painted white. She is seen her at Largs, berthed along the south side of the pier.

Talisman alongside Millport Old Pier on 1 August 1961.

Talisman with a good number on board, arriving at Millport. In addition to the Millport ferry service she offered Sunday afternoon sailings from Millport and Largs to Tighnabruiach.

In 1965, *Talisman* received a red lion on her funnel, along with the remainder of the CSP fleet, and her hull was painted 'monastral blue'.

Talisman arriving at Rothesay on 25 July 1965. The Millport roster included afternoon sailings from Millport to Rothesay which were marketed as 'Cumbrae Circle Cruises'.

Talisman made her final passenger sailing on 17 November 1966, as a tender to the CPR liner *Empress of Scotland*. After lay up in Greenock's East India Harbour, on 17 October 1967 she was towed up river to Arnott Young's Dalmuir shipbreaking yard, where she ended her days.

Twelve
Waverley of 1947

In 1945 the LNER ordered a second *Waverley* from A & J Inglis to replace Waverley and Marmion. She was launched on 2 October 1946 and entered service in June 1947. She is seen here on her first day in service, 16 June 1947.

Another view of *Waverley* on the same day, with *Jeanie Deans* ahead of her. Her LNER colours differed from her Waverley Steam Navigation colours prior to 2000 in that the deck saloons in LNER days were finished in grained wood.

CLYDE STEAMER, P.S. "WAVERLEY"   B 9930

In 1953 the ownership of the three ex-LNER steamers was transferred from British Railways to the Caledonian Steam Packet Co., thus circumventing the restrictions on railway-owned steamers visiting some of the more far-flung Clyde piers such as Inveraray or Campbeltown. *Waverley* is seen here in the Firth of Clyde between 1953, when her brown deckhouses were painted white, and 1959 when her paddle boxes were painted white.

On Fridays from the late fifties until the late sixties, *Waverley* undertook an up-river sailing from Largs to Glasgow Bridge Wharf, where she is seen here.

Waverley in the 1950's with black paddle boxes, which were repainted white in 1959. The ring on her funnels, which separated the white band from the red lower part in the LNER colours, can be seen. *Waverley* received new funnels in 1961 and 1962 respectively.

In 1965 *Waverley* received lions on her funnels and, until the end of the 1969 season, a 'monastral blue' hull. She is seen her off Brodick.

Waverley at Dunoon in summer 1968, with *Duchess of Hamilton* arriving at the pier.

Waverley at Rothesay in the late sixties.

Waverley at Craigendoran in the summer of 1968, with the *Caledonia* on the right.

Waverley, having just left Innellan for Dunoon, in a view taken shortly after the previous photograph.

Waverley at Tighnabruaich in 1965-1969 colours.

Waverley visited Ardrishaig on a Clyde River Steamer Club North British Centenary charter from Gourock and Helensburgh on 16 April 1965.

Waverley, with *Queen Mary II* behind her and the stern of *Duchess of Hamilton* forward of *Queen Mary II*, in winter lay-up in Queens Dock in the 1967-1968 winter. This dock is now filled in and covered by the SECC.

Finished with Engines. *Waverley's* funnels, covered with tarpaulins, while in winter lay-up in Rothesay Dock, 1968-1969.

Waverley and *Caledonia* in Rothesay Dock, 1968-1969. The funnels in the right background belong to hopper barges.

In 1970, following the formation of the Scottish Transport Group, *Waverley's* hull was painted black again.

In 1973, after an abortive attempt to paint the funnels red, with a yellow stripe and black top, Waverley received standard Caledonian MacBrayne funnels of red with black tops and a yellow disc surrounding the lions. Her paddle boxes were repainted black with a white surround.

Thirteen
Waverley in preservation

Waverley was withdrawn by Caledonian MacBrayne after the 1973 season, and on 8 August 1974, was sold for the nominal sum of £1 to the Waverley Steam Navigation Company, a company set up by the Paddle Steamer Preservation Society to operate her. She re-entered service on 22 May 1975.

The new owners of *Waverley* used every opportunity to publicise and market her sailings. Here, on 4 July 1976, America's Bicentennial Independence Day, she sports silver stars on her funnels and flies the Stars and Stripes from her foremast. This photograph was taken at Anderston Quay, Glasgow.

Waverley leaving Greenock up-river.

Unusual calls at seldom-visited piers have been a feature of *Waverley's* years in preservation. Here she is seen at Kilmun on a Paddle Steamer Preservation Society charter in September 1979, with Western Ferries *Sound of Sanda*, ex-*Lymington*, berthed alongside on her far side.

Another unusual call later on the same cruise in 1979 was at Ardyne, a short-lived oil rig construction yard across from Rothesay on the Cowal shore.

Another unusual call, this time a scheduled one, was at Portencross on Easter Sunday 1995. This was the first call at this privately owned pier by a Clyde steamer since before 1914.

Inveraray has been an occasional call for *Waverley*, seen here on a special trip in 1976 from the top of the Bell Tower.

Iona has always been a favoured destination from Oban, sometimes retracing the route round Mull of the *King George V*, outwards via Tobermory and passing close to Staffa, but, more often, starting the day at Fort William and sailing both ways by the south of Mull. Whichever way, *Waverley* has to anchor in the sound of Iona and is tendered by small craft to let the passengers ashore. She is seen here in 1998.

Waverley's first foray out of the Firth of Clyde was for a short series of sailings from Liverpool in early May 1977. *Waverley* is seen here at Liverpool Landing Stage.

Waverley has been an annual visitor to the Bristol Channel since 1979. She is seen here on 2 June 1979 at Ilfracombe, with *Balmoral*, still in P & A Campbell ownership, moored forward of her.

Waverley, boarded up for the light voyage round Lands End, at St Ives, on an occasion in 1979 when she had to put in there because of a stormy weather forecast for the trip round Lands End.

Waverley at Bournemouth Pier in September 1982.

Waverley at Southampton's Royal Pier on her first visit there in 1978 with Blue Funnel Cruises docks excursion boat *Portsea.*.

In 1978, *Waverley* paid her visit to the Thames, with a more successful short season than her ex-fleetmate *Queen of the South*, ex-*Jeanie Deans*, had had a dozen years earlier.

A view of *Waverley's* undersides in dry dock, photographed on a PSPS visit to *Waverley* in Govan dry dock in the 1978-1979 winter.

Waverley has often rendezvoused with cruise ships visiting the Clyde, and is seen here in 1998 with the *Norway*, formerly the transatlantic liner *France* of French Line.

In 1981 and 1982, Waverley visited the Forth. She is seen here approaching the Forth Rail Bridge in the latter year.

On 21 December 1999, *Waverley* arrived at the yard of George Prior Engineering Ltd in Great Yarmouth for her millennium rebuild. By early January the aft funnel and fidlee casing underneath it had been removed and work was starting on dismantling the sponsons and paddles. (SC)

By 8 February 2000, *Waverley's* engine had been dismantled, boilers, sponsons and aft deckhouse removed, and she was towed to Richards dry-dock on the opposite bank of the River Yare. (SC)

In June, the triple expansion engines were being reassembled, with the crankshaft seen here being placed back in position. (SC)

By late July, *Waverley* had had her new funnels fitted, her hull painted in a grey undercoat, and her upperworks painted cream. The paddlebox still had to be fitted. (SC)

In May 2000, *Waverley's* new port boiler is being lifted aboard. Twin boilers were fitted in the 2000 rebuild, rather than the single boiler used previously. They were manufactured by Cochran Boilers of Annan. (SC)

Waverley returned from her £4m rebuild at Great Yarmouth on 18 August 2000, and operated an evening cruise on that day. She is seen here passing Renfrew Ferry on 19 August, her first full day in service following her rebuild. Note that the deckhouses and ventilators are now painted brown, as in her original season of 1947. Note also the housing for the new emergency exit from the dining saloon on the aft deck, above the rearmost small square window.

Waverley's dining saloon was completely refitted during her rebuild with an attempt to be as near as possible to the original furnishings of 1947. The lower dining saloon at the bottom of the stairs in the centre is now open to the public and similarly furnished, having previously been a store.

Waverley's engine room in 2000. Her triple-expansion machinery, built by Rankin and Blackmore at the Eagle Foundry, Greenock, was totally dismantled and refitted during her rebuild.

Waverley approaching Largs, 22 August 2000.

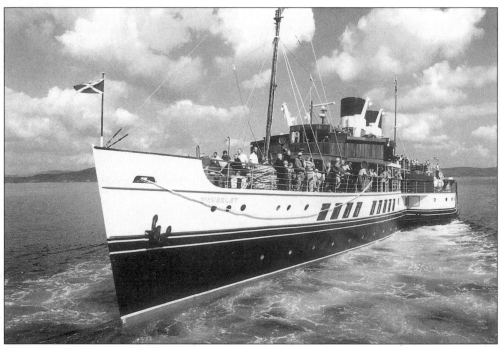

Waverley reversing out of Tarbert, Loch Fyne on 22 August 2000, during her short Clyde season in that year.